HUNT.
FISH.
COLOR!

Original Pen & Ink Artwork by Brenda Potts

www.BooksByPotts.com

Cover Illustration by rudall30 of
ThinkstockPhotos.com by Getty Images, iStock Collection

ISBN 978-0-9883272-3-8

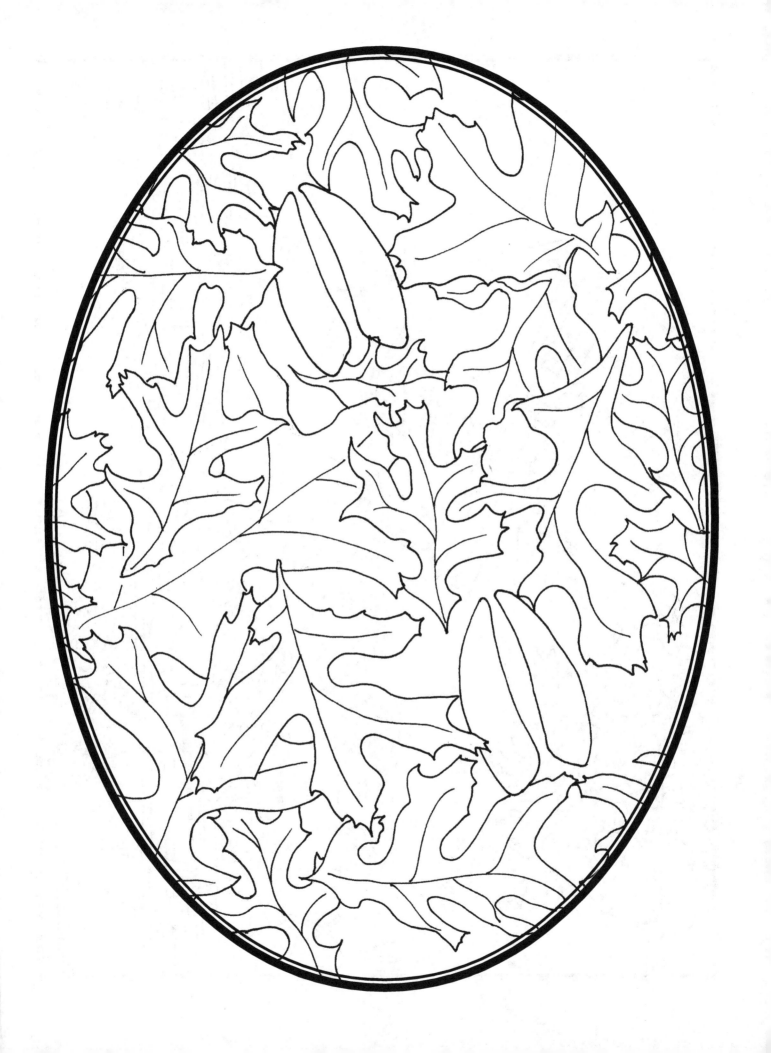

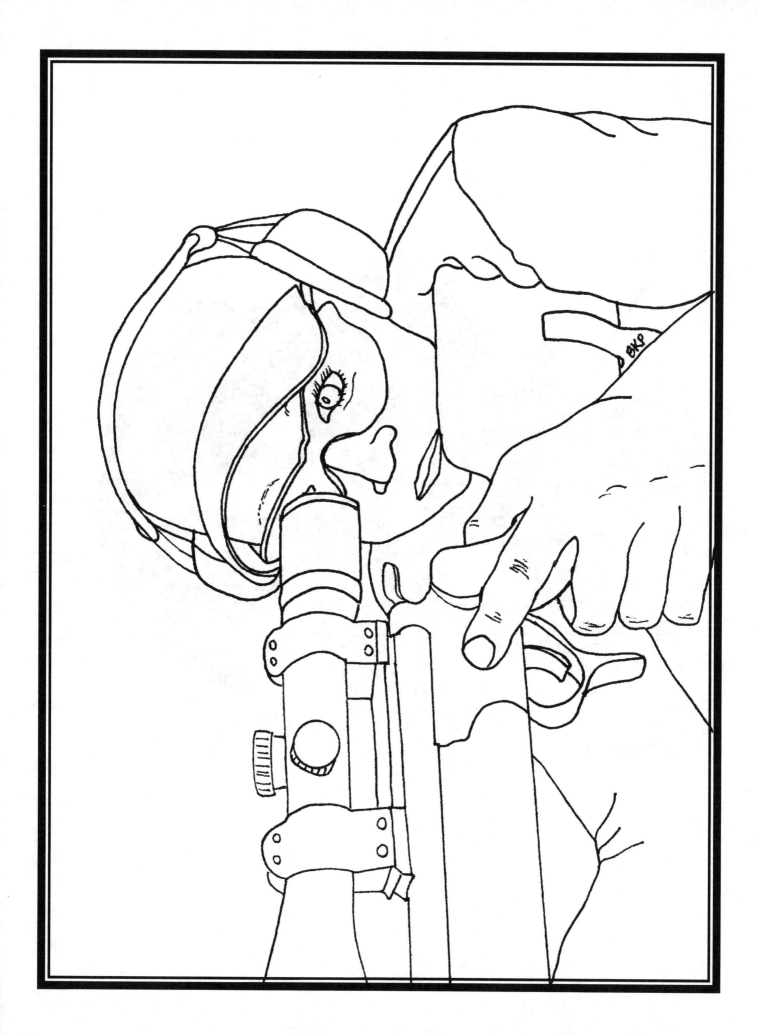

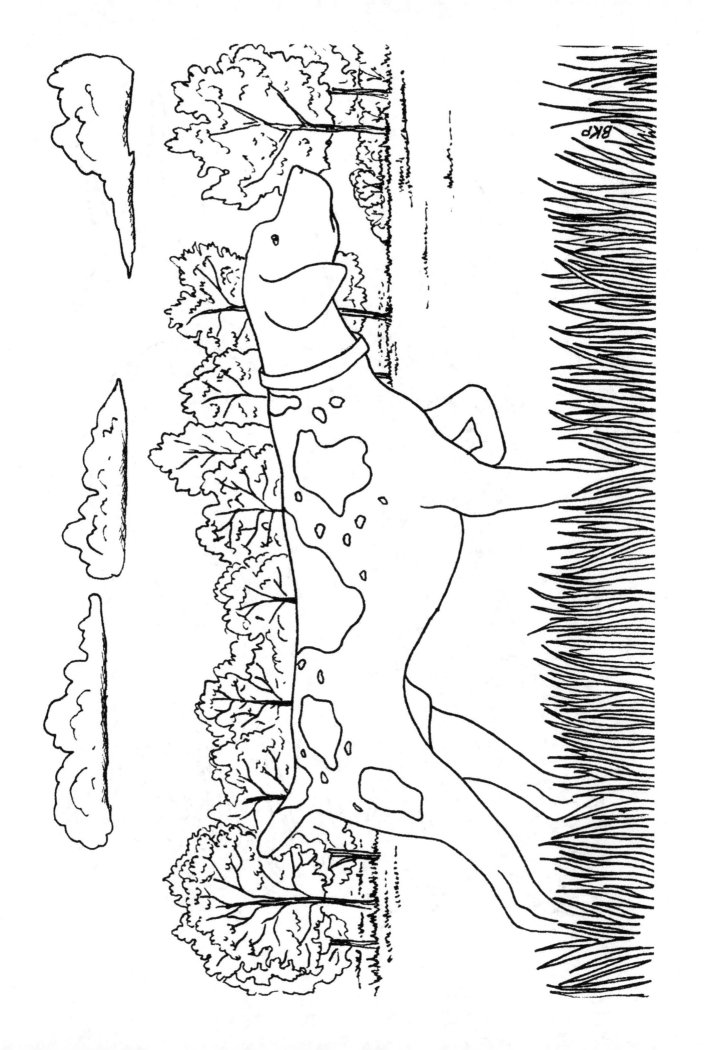

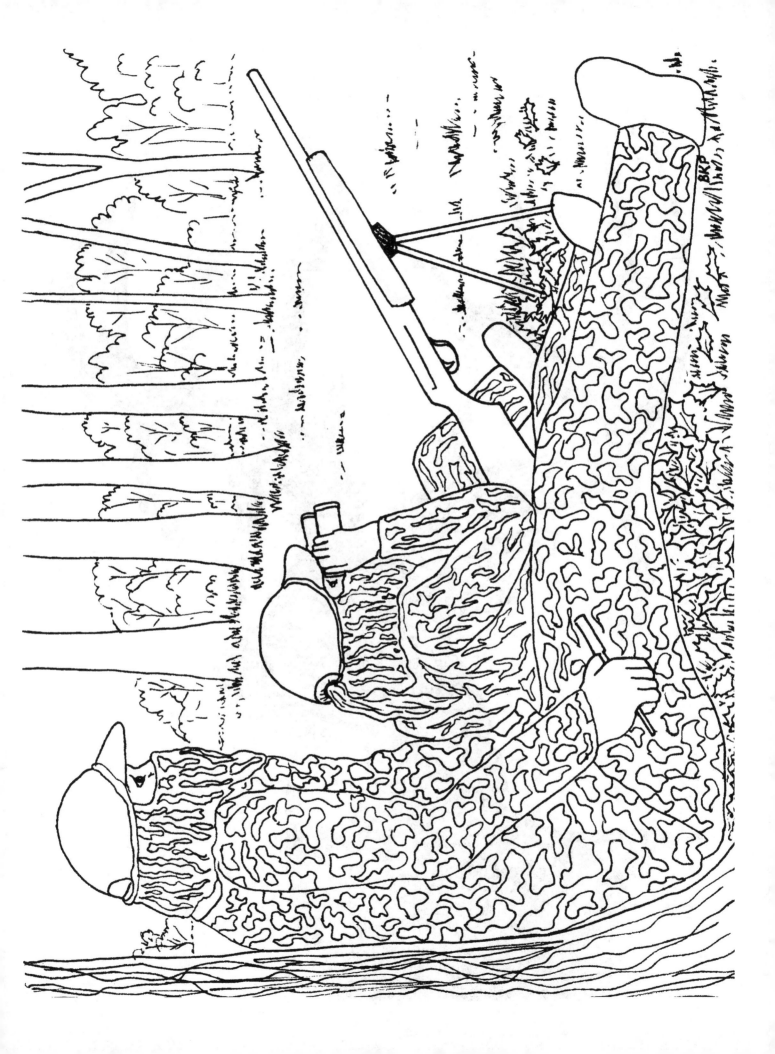

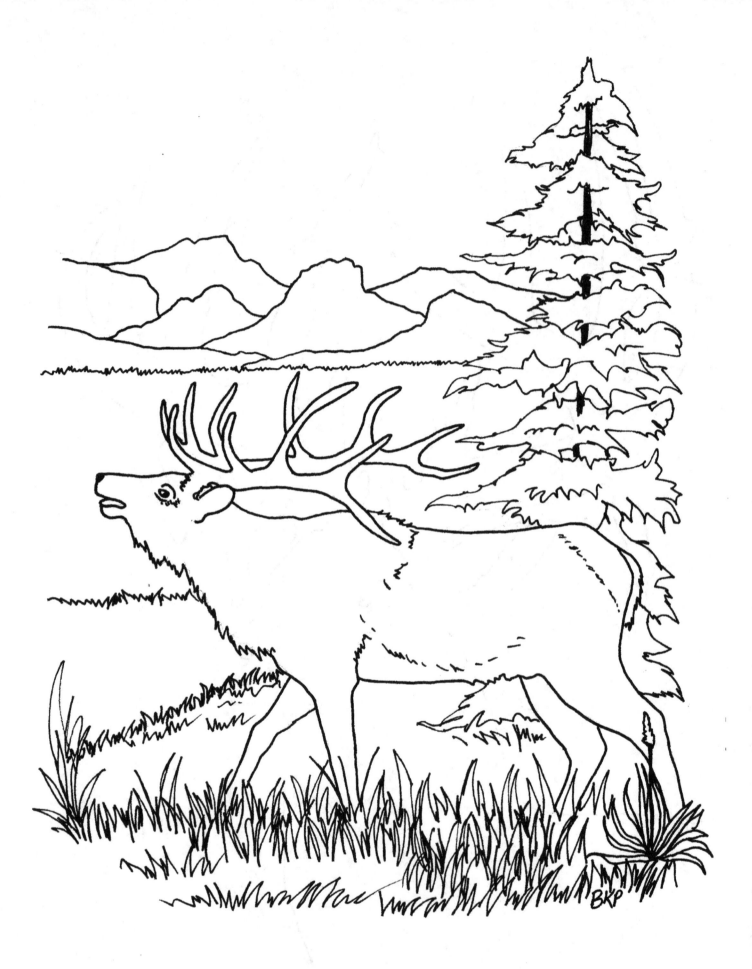

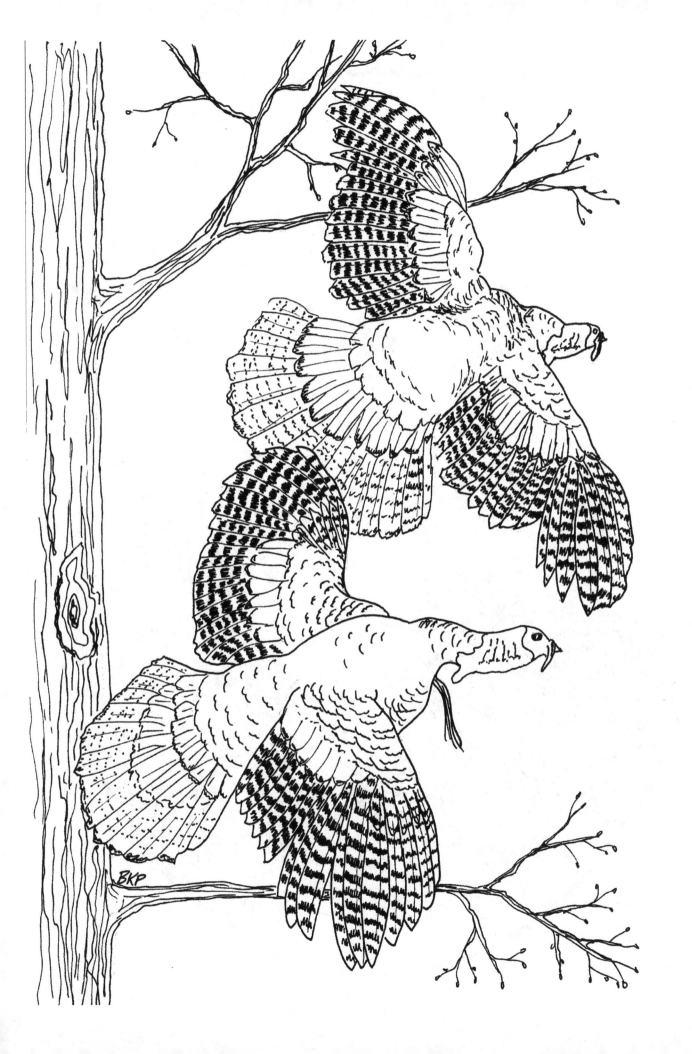

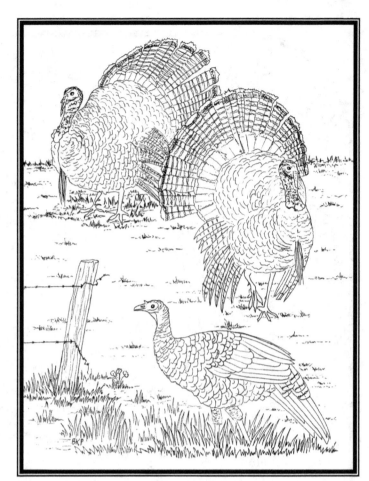

CPSIA information can be obtained
at www.ICGtesting.com
Printed in the USA
BVHW011146081118
532533BV00012B/168/P